SOLAS

AMENDMENTS 2010 and 2011

INTERNATIONAL
MARITIME
ORGANIZATION

London, 2011

Published in 2011
by the INTERNATIONAL MARITIME ORGANIZATION
4 Albert Embankment, London SE1 7SR
www.imo.org

Printed by CPI Group (UK) Ltd, Croydon, CR0 4YY

PEFC/06-37-03

ISBN: 978-92-801-1542-0

IMO PUBLICATION
Sales number: I176E

This publication has been prepared from official documents of IMO, and every effort
has been made to eliminate errors and reproduce the original text(s) faithfully. Readers
should be aware that, in case of inconsistency, the official IMO text will prevail.

022080

Contents

Foreword

This publication contains the amendments to the International Convention for the Safety of Life at Sea (SOLAS) 1974 and the 1988 SOLAS Protocol adopted by the Maritime Safety Committee (MSC) at its eighty-seventh, eighty-eighth and eighty-ninth sessions in 2010 and 2011.

Resolution MSC.290(87) was adopted by MSC 87 in May 2010 and contains amendments to SOLAS regulation II-1/2 and new regulation II-1/3-10 (Goal-based Ship Construction Standards for Bulk Carriers and Oil Tankers), making the International Goal-based Ship Construction Standards for Bulk Carriers and Oil Tankers (resolution MSC.287(87)), which describe the goals and establish functional requirements that rules for the design and construction of bulk carriers and oil tankers shall conform to, mandatory under the SOLAS Convention.

Resolution MSC.291(87) was also adopted by MSC 87 and contains new SOLAS regulation II-1/3-11 (Corrosion protection of cargo oil tanks of crude oil tankers), as well as amendments to chapter II-2, regulations 1 (Application) and 4 (Probability of ignition). New regulation II-1/3-11 introduces requirements for corrosion protection of the cargo oil tanks of crude oil tankers and makes the Performance Standard for protective coatings for cargo oil tanks of crude oil tankers (resolution MSC.288(87)) and the Performance Standard for alternative means of corrosion protection for cargo oil tanks of crude oil tankers (resolution MSC.289(87)), mandatory under the SOLAS Convention. The amendments to regulation II-2/4 concern gas measurement and detection in double-hull and double-bottom spaces.

Resolution MSC.308(88) was adopted by MSC 88 in December 2010 and contains amendments to SOLAS chapters II-1, II-2, V and to the appendix (Certificates). The amendments, in particular:

    .1   clarify the application requirements in chapters II-1 and II-2;

    .2   make the International Code for Application of Fire Test Procedures, 2010 (2010 FTP Code) (resolution MSC.307(88)), mandatory under the SOLAS Convention;

.3 update and improve regulation V/23 (Pilot transfer arrangements); and

.4 introduce documentation of alternative design and arrangements in the SOLAS certificate forms.

Resolution MSC.309(88) was also adopted by MSC 88 and contains amendments to the 1988 Protocol to introduce documentation of alternative design and arrangements in the SOLAS certificate forms, corresponding to the associated amendments to the SOLAS Convention, adopted by resolution MSC.308(88).

Resolution MSC.317(89) was adopted by MSC 89 in May 2011 and contains an amendment to SOLAS regulation III/1, mandating the replacement of on-load release mechanisms not complying with the relevant provisions of the Life-saving Appliance (LSA) Code, not later than the first scheduled dry-docking after 1 July 2014. Guidance on the matter is provided in the Guidelines for evaluation and replacement of lifeboat release and retrieval systems (MSC/Circ.1392).

Amendments, by SOLAS chapter

Chapter	Resolution	Page in Publication
II-1 Construction – Structure, subdivision and stability, machinery and electrical installations	MSC.290(87) (annex 4) MSC.291(87) (annex 5) MSC.308(88) (annex 2)	5–7 11–12 17
II-2 Construction – Fire protection, fire detection and fire extinction	MSC.291(87) (annex 5) MSC.308(88) (annex 2)	13–14 17–19
III Life-saving appliances and arrangements	MSC.317(89) (annex 1)	35
V Safety of navigation	MSC.308(88) (annex 2)	19–24
Appendix – Certificates	MSC.308(88) (annex 2) MSC.309(88) (annex 3)	24–25 29–30

2010 amendments

The amendments presented in this section comprise the annexes to resolutions MSC.290(87) and MSC.291(87) adopted in May 2010, and MSC.308(88) and MSC.309(88) adopted in December 2010. See the individual resolutions for information on the respective amendments' acceptance and entry into force.

Resolution MSC.290(87)

(adopted on 21 May 2010)

Adoption of amendments to the International Convention for the Safety of Life at Sea, 1974, as amended

THE MARITIME SAFETY COMMITTEE,

RECALLING Article 28(b) of the Convention on the International Maritime Organization concerning the functions of the Committee,

RECALLING ALSO article VIII(b) of the International Convention for the Safety of Life at Sea (SOLAS), 1974 (hereinafter referred to as "the Convention"), concerning the amendment procedure applicable to the Annex to the Convention, other than to the provisions of chapter I thereof,

RECALLING FURTHER that among the strategic directions of the Organization relating to developing and maintaining a comprehensive framework for safe, secure, efficient and environmentally sound shipping is the establishment of goal-based standards for the design and construction of new ships,

CONSIDERING that ships should be designed and constructed for a specified design life to be safe and environmentally friendly, so that, if properly operated and maintained under specified operating and environmental conditions, they can remain safe throughout their service life,

HAVING CONSIDERED, at its eighty-seventh session, amendments to the Convention, proposed and circulated in accordance with article VIII(b)(i) thereof,

1.   ADOPTS, in accordance with article VIII(b)(iv) of the Convention, amendments to the Convention, the text of which is set out in the Annex to the present resolution;

2.   DETERMINES, in accordance with article VIII(b)(vi)(2)(bb) of the Convention, that the said amendments shall be deemed to have been accepted on 1 July 2011, unless, prior to that date, more than one third of the Contracting Governments to the Convention or Contracting Governments the combined merchant fleets of which constitute not less than 50% of the gross tonnage of the world's merchant fleet, have notified their objections to the amendments;

3.   INVITES SOLAS Contracting Governments to note that, in accordance with article VIII(b)(vii)(2) of the Convention, the amendments shall enter into force on 1 January 2012 upon their acceptance in accordance with paragraph 2 above;

4.   REQUESTS the Secretary-General, in conformity with article VIII(b)(v) of the Convention, to transmit certified copies of the present resolution and the text of the amendments contained in the Annex to all Contracting Governments to the Convention;

5.   FURTHER REQUESTS the Secretary-General to transmit copies of this resolution and its Annex to Members of the Organization which are not Contracting Governments to the Convention;

6.   RESOLVES to review the progress towards the implementation of SOLAS regulation II 1/3-10 in 2014 and, if proven necessary, to adjust the time periods set forth in paragraph 1 of the regulation.

Annex

Amendments to the International Convention for the Safety of Life at Sea, 1974, as amended

Chapter II-1
Construction – Structure, subdivision and stability,
machinery and electrical installations

Part A
General

Regulation 2
Definitions

1   *The following new paragraph 28 is added after the existing paragraph 27:*

"**28**   *Goal-based Ship Construction Standards for Bulk Carriers and Oil Tankers* means the International Goal-Based Ship Construction Standards for Bulk Carriers and Oil Tankers, adopted by the Maritime Safety Committee by resolution MSC.287(87), as may be amended by the Organization, provided that such amendments are adopted, brought into force and take effect in accordance with the provisions of article VIII of the present Convention concerning the amendment procedures applicable to the annex other than chapter I thereof."

Part A-1
Structure of ships

2   The following new regulation 3-10 is added after the existing regulation 3-9:

"Regulation 3-10
Goal-based ship construction standards for bulk carriers and oil tankers

1   This regulation shall apply to oil tankers of 150 m in length and above and to bulk carriers of 150 m in length and above, constructed with single deck, top-side tanks and hopper side tanks in cargo spaces, excluding ore carriers and combination carriers:

    .1   for which the building contract is placed on or after 1 July 2016;

    .2   in the absence of a building contract, the keels of which are laid or which are at a similar stage of construction on or after 1 July 2017; or

    .3   the delivery of which is on or after 1 July 2020.

2   Ships shall be designed and constructed for a specified design life to be safe and environmentally friendly, when properly operated and maintained under the specified operating and environmental conditions, in intact and specified damage conditions, throughout their life.

2.1   *Safe and environmentally friendly* means the ship shall have adequate strength, integrity and stability to minimize the risk of loss of the ship or pollution to the marine environment due to structural failure, including collapse, resulting in flooding or loss of watertight integrity.

2.2   *Environmentally friendly* also includes the ship being constructed of materials for environmentally acceptable recycling.

2.3   *Safety* also includes the ship's structure, fittings and arrangements providing for safe access, escape, inspection and proper maintenance and facilitating safe operation.

2.4   *Specified operating and environmental conditions* are defined by the intended operating area for the ship throughout its life and cover the conditions, including intermediate conditions, arising from cargo and ballast operations in port, waterways and at sea.

2.5 *Specified design life* is the nominal period that the ship is assumed to be exposed to operating and/or environmental conditions and/or the corrosive environment and is used for selecting appropriate ship design parameters. However, the ship's actual service life may be longer or shorter depending on the actual operating conditions and maintenance of the ship throughout its life cycle.

3   The requirements of paragraphs 2 to 2.5 shall be achieved through satisfying applicable structural requirements of an organization which is recognized by the Administration in accordance with the provisions of regulation XI-1/1, or national standards of the Administration, conforming to the functional requirements of the Goal-based Ship Construction Standards for Bulk Carriers and Oil Tankers.

4   A Ship Construction File with specific information on how the functional requirements of the Goal-based Ship Construction Standards for Bulk Carriers and Oil Tankers have been applied in the ship design and construction shall be provided upon delivery of a new ship, and kept on board the ship and/or ashore and updated as appropriate throughout the ship's service. The contents of the Ship Construction File shall, at least, conform to the guidelines developed by the Organization.[*]

---

[*] Refer to the Guidelines for the information to be included in a Ship Construction File (MSC.1/Circ.1343)."

Resolution MSC.291(87)

(adopted on 21 May 2010)

Adoption of amendments to the International Convention for the Safety of Life at Sea, 1974, as amended

THE MARITIME SAFETY COMMITTEE,

RECALLING Article 28(b) of the Convention on the International Maritime Organization concerning the functions of the Committee,

RECALLING FURTHER article VIII(b) of the International Convention for the Safety of Life at Sea (SOLAS), 1974 (hereinafter referred to as "the Convention"), concerning the amendment procedure applicable to the Annex to the Convention, other than to the provisions of chapter I thereof,

HAVING CONSIDERED, at its eighty-seventh session, amendments to the Convention, proposed and circulated in accordance with article VIII(b)(i) thereof,

1.   ADOPTS, in accordance with article VIII(b)(iv) of the Convention, amendments to the Convention, the text of which is set out in the Annex to the present resolution;

2.   DETERMINES, in accordance with article VIII(b)(vi)(2)(bb) of the Convention, that the said amendments shall be deemed to have been accepted on 1 July 2011, unless, prior to that date, more than one third of the Contracting Governments to the Convention or Contracting Governments the combined merchant fleets of which constitute not less than 50% of the gross tonnage of the world's merchant fleet, have notified their objections to the amendments;

3.   INVITES SOLAS Contracting Governments to note that, in accordance with article VIII(b)(vii)(2) of the Convention, the amendments shall

9

enter into force on 1 January 2012 upon their acceptance in accordance with paragraph 2 above;

4.   REQUESTS the Secretary-General, in conformity with article VIII(b)(v) of the Convention, to transmit certified copies of the present resolution and the text of the amendments contained in the Annex to all Contracting Governments to the Convention;

5.   FURTHER REQUESTS the Secretary-General to transmit copies of this resolution and its Annex to Members of the Organization, which are not Contracting Governments to the Convention.

Annex

Amendments to the International Convention for the Safety of Life at Sea, 1974, as amended

Chapter II-1
Construction – Structure, subdivision and stability, machinery and electrical installations

Part A-1
Structure of ships

1   *The following new regulation 3-11 is added after regulation 3-10:*

"Regulation 3-11
Corrosion protection of cargo oil tanks of crude oil tankers

1   Paragraph 3 shall apply to crude oil tankers,[*] as defined in regulation 1 of Annex I to the International Convention for the Prevention of Pollution from Ships, 1973, as modified by the Protocol of 1978 relating thereto, of 5,000 tonnes deadweight and above:

    .1   for which the building contract is placed on or after 1 January 2013; or

    .2   in the absence of a building contract, the keels of which are laid or which are at a similar stage of construction on or after 1 July 2013; or

    .3   the delivery of which is on or after 1 January 2016.

2   Paragraph 3 shall not apply to combination carriers or chemical tankers as defined in regulations 1 of Annexes I and II, respectively, to the International Convention for the Prevention of Pollution from Ships, 1973, as modified by the Protocol of 1978 relating thereto. For the purpose of this regulation, chemical tankers also include chemical tankers certified to carry oil.

---

[*] Refer to items 1.11.1 or 1.11.4 of the Supplement to the International Oil Pollution Prevention Certificate (Form B).

3   All cargo oil tanks of crude oil tankers shall be:

    .1   coated during the construction of the ship in accordance with the Performance standard for protective coatings for cargo oil tanks of crude oil tankers, adopted by the Maritime Safety Committee by resolution MSC.288(87), as may be amended by the Organization, provided that such amendments are adopted, brought into force and take effect in accordance with the provisions of article VIII of the present Convention concerning the amendment procedures applicable to the Annex other than chapter I; or

    .2   protected by alternative means of corrosion protection or utilization of corrosion resistance material to maintain required structural integrity for 25 years in accordance with the Performance standard for alternative means of corrosion protection for cargo oil tanks of crude oil tankers, adopted by the Maritime Safety Committee by resolution MSC.289(87), as may be amended by the Organization, provided that such amendments are adopted, brought into force and take effect in accordance with the provisions of article VIII of the present Convention concerning the amendment procedures applicable to the Annex other than chapter I.

4   The Administration may exempt a crude oil tanker from the requirements of paragraph 3 to allow the use of novel prototype alternatives to the coating system specified in paragraph 3.1, for testing, provided they are subject to suitable controls, regular assessment and acknowledgement of the need for immediate remedial action if the system fails or is shown to be failing. Such exemption shall be recorded on an exemption certificate.

5   The Administration may exempt a crude oil tanker from the requirements of paragraph 3 if the ship is built to be engaged solely in the carriage of cargoes and cargo handling operations not causing corrosion.* Such exemption and conditions for which it is granted shall be recorded on an exemption certificate.

---

* Refer to the guidelines to be developed by the Organization."

Chapter II-2
Construction – Fire protection, fire detection and fire extinction

Part A
General

Regulation 1
Application

2   *In paragraph 2.2, in subparagraph .4, the word "*and*" is deleted; in subparagraph .5 the word "*and*" is added at the end; and the following new subparagraph .6 is added after the existing subparagraph .5:*

".**6**   regulation 4.5.7.1."

Part B
Prevention of fire and explosion

Regulation 4
Probability of ignition

3   *The existing paragraph 5.7 is replaced by the following:*

"5.7 Gas measurement and detection

5.7.1 Portable instrument

Tankers shall be equipped with at least one portable instrument for measuring oxygen and one for measuring flammable vapour concentrations, together with a sufficient set of spares. Suitable means shall be provided for the calibration of such instruments.

5.7.2 Arrangements for gas measurement in double-hull spaces and double-bottom spaces

5.7.2.1 Suitable portable instruments for measuring oxygen and flammable vapour concentrations in double-hull spaces and double-bottom spaces shall be provided. In selecting these instruments, due attention shall be given to their use in combination with the fixed gas sampling line systems referred to in paragraph 5.7.2.2.

5.7.2.2 Where the atmosphere in double-hull spaces cannot be reliably measured using flexible gas sampling hoses, such spaces shall be fitted with permanent gas sampling lines. The configuration of gas sampling lines shall be adapted to the design of such spaces.

5.7.2.3 The materials of construction and dimensions of gas sampling lines shall be such as to prevent restriction. Where plastic materials are used, they shall be electrically conductive.

5.7.3 Arrangements for fixed hydrocarbon gas detection systems in double hull and double-bottom spaces of oil tankers

5.7.3.1 In addition to the requirements in paragraphs 5.7.1 and 5.7.2, oil tankers of 20,000 tonnes deadweight and above, constructed on or after 1 January 2012, shall be provided with a fixed hydrocarbon gas detection system complying with the Fire Safety Systems Code for measuring hydrocarbon gas concentrations in all ballast tanks and void spaces of double-hull and double-bottom spaces adjacent to the cargo tanks, including the forepeak tank and any other tanks and spaces under the bulkhead deck adjacent to cargo tanks.

5.7.3.2 Oil tankers provided with constant operative inerting systems for such spaces need not be equipped with fixed hydrocarbon gas detection equipment.

5.7.3.3 Notwithstanding the above, cargo pump-rooms subject to the provisions of paragraph 5.10 need not comply with the requirements of this paragraph."

Resolution MSC.308(88)

(adopted on 3 December 2010)

Amendments to the International Convention for the safety of life at sea, 1974, as amended

THE MARITIME SAFETY COMMITTEE,

RECALLING Article 28(b) of the Convention on the International Maritime Organization concerning the functions of the Committee,

RECALLING FURTHER article VIII(b) of the International Convention for the Safety of Life at Sea (SOLAS), 1974 (hereinafter referred to as "the Convention"), concerning the amendment procedure applicable to the Annex to the Convention, other than to the provisions of chapter I thereof,

HAVING CONSIDERED, at its eighty-eighth session, amendments to the Convention, proposed and circulated in accordance with article VIII(b)(i) thereof,

1.   ADOPTS, in accordance with article VIII(b)(iv) of the Convention, amendments to the Convention, the text of which is set out in the Annex to the present resolution;

2.   DETERMINES, in accordance with article VIII(b)(vi)(2)(bb) of the Convention, that the said amendments shall be deemed to have been accepted on 1 January 2012, unless, prior to that date, more than one third of the Contracting Governments to the Convention or Contracting Governments the combined merchant fleets of which constitute not less than 50% of the gross tonnage of the world's merchant fleet, have notified their objections to the amendments;

3.   INVITES SOLAS Contracting Governments to note that, in accordance with article VIII(b)(vii)(2) of the Convention, the amendments shall enter into force on 1 July 2012 upon their acceptance in accordance with paragraph 2 above;

4.   REQUESTS the Secretary-General, in conformity with article VIII(b)(v) of the Convention, to transmit certified copies of the present resolution and the text of the amendments contained in the Annex to all Contracting Governments to the Convention;

5.   FURTHER REQUESTS the Secretary-General to transmit copies of this resolution and its Annex to Members of the Organization which are not Contracting Governments to the Convention.

Annex

Amendments to the International Convention for the Safety of Life at Sea, 1974, as amended

Chapter II-1
Construction – Structure, subdivision and stability,
machinery and electrical installations

Part D
Electrical installations

Regulation 41
Main source of electrical power and lighting systems

1   *In paragraph 6, the words* "constructed on or after 1 July 2010" *are inserted after the words* "In passenger ships".

Chapter II-2
Construction – Fire protection, fire detection
and fire extinction

Part A
General

Regulation 1
Application

2   *In paragraph 1.1, the date* "1 July 2002" *is replaced by the date* "1 July 2012".

3   *In paragraph 1.2.2, the date "1 July 2002" is replaced by the date "1 July 2012".*

4   *The existing paragraph 2.1 is replaced by the following:*

"**2.1** Unless expressly provided otherwise, for ships constructed before 1 July 2012, the Administration shall ensure that the requirements which are applicable under chapter II-2 of the International Convention for the Safety of Life at Sea, 1974, as amended by resolutions MSC.1(XLV), MSC.6(48), MSC.13(57), MSC.22(59), MSC.24(60), MSC.27(61), MSC.31(63), MSC.57(67), MSC.99(73), MSC.134(76), MSC.194(80), MSC.201(81), MSC.216(82), MSC.256(84), MSC.269(85) and MSC.291(87) are complied with."

5   *In paragraph 3.1, the date "1 July 2002" is replaced by the date "1 July 2012".*

6   *In paragraph 3.2, the date "1 July 2002" is replaced by the date "1 July 2012".*

Regulation 3
Definitions

7   *The existing paragraph 23 is replaced by the following:*

"**23** Fire Test Procedures Code means the International Code for Application of Fire Test Procedures, 2010 (2010 FTP Code) as adopted by the Maritime Safety Committee of the Organization by resolution MSC.307(88), as may be amended by the Organization, provided that such amendments are adopted, brought into force and take effect in accordance with the provisions of article VIII of the present Convention concerning the amendment procedures applicable to the Annex other than chapter I."

Part C
Suppression of fire

Regulation 7
Detection and alarm

8   *In paragraph 4.1, at the end of subparagraph .1, the word "*and*" is deleted; at the end of subparagraph .2.2, the period "*.*" is replaced by the word "*; and*"; and the following new subparagraph .3 is added after the existing subparagraph .2.2:*

> ".3   enclosed spaces containing incinerators."

Chapter V
Safety of navigation

Regulation 18
Approval, surveys and performance standards
of navigation systems and equipment
and voyage data recorder

9   *The following new paragraph 9 is added after the existing paragraph 8:*

> "9   The automatic identification system (AIS) shall be subjected to an annual test. The test shall be conducted by an approved surveyor or an approved testing or servicing facility. The test shall verify the correct programming of the ship static information, correct data exchange with connected sensors as well as verifying the radio performance by radio frequency measurement and on-air test using, e.g., a Vessel Traffic Service (VTS). A copy of the test report shall be retained on board the ship."

Regulation 23
Pilot transfer arrangements

10   *The existing text of regulation 23 is replaced by the following:*

"1   Application

1.1   Ships engaged on voyages in the course of which pilots may be employed shall be provided with pilot transfer arrangements.

1.2   Equipment and arrangements for pilot transfer which are installed[*] on or after 1 July 2012 shall comply with the requirements of this regulation, and due regard shall be paid to the standards adopted by the Organization.[†]

1.3   Except as provided otherwise, equipment and arrangements for pilot transfer which are provided on ships before 1 July 2012 shall at least comply with the requirements of regulation 17[‡] or 23, as applicable, of the Convention in force prior to that date, and due regard shall be paid to the standards adopted by the Organization prior to that date.

1.4   Equipment and arrangements installed on or after 1 July 2012, which are a replacement of equipment and arrangements provided on ships before 1 July 2012, shall, in so far as is reasonable and practicable, comply with the requirements of this regulation.

1.5   With respect to ships constructed before 1 January 1994, paragraph 5 shall apply not later than the first survey[§] on or after 1 July 2012.

1.6   Paragraph 6 applies to all ships.

2   General

2.1   All arrangements used for pilot transfer shall efficiently fulfil their purpose of enabling pilots to embark and disembark safely. The appliances shall be kept clean, properly maintained and stowed and shall be regularly

---

[*] Refer to the Unified interpretation of SOLAS regulation V/23 (MSC.1/Circ.1375).

[†] Refer to the Pilot transfer arrangements, adopted by the Organization by resolution A.1045(27).

[‡] Refer to resolution MSC.99(73), renumbering previous regulation 17 as regulation 23, which entered into force on 1 July 2002.

[§] Refer to the Unified interpretation of the term "first survey" referred to in SOLAS regulations (MSC.1/Circ.1290).

inspected to ensure that they are safe to use. They shall be used solely for the embarkation and disembarkation of personnel.

2.2 The rigging of the pilot transfer arrangements and the embarkation of a pilot shall be supervised by a responsible officer having means of communication with the navigation bridge and who shall also arrange for the escort of the pilot by a safe route to and from the navigation bridge. Personnel engaged in rigging and operating any mechanical equipment shall be instructed in the safe procedures to be adopted and the equipment shall be tested prior to use.

2.3 A pilot ladder shall be certified by the manufacturer as complying with this regulation or with an international standard acceptable to the Organization.[*] Ladders shall be inspected in accordance with regulations I/6, 7 and 8.

2.4 All pilot ladders used for pilot transfer shall be clearly identified with tags or other permanent marking so as to enable identification of each appliance for the purposes of survey, inspection and record keeping. A record shall be kept on the ship as to the date the identified ladder is placed into service and any repairs effected.

2.5 Reference in this regulation to an accommodation ladder includes a sloping ladder used as part of the pilot transfer arrangements.

3 Transfer arrangements

3.1 Arrangements shall be provided to enable the pilot to embark and disembark safely on either side of the ship.

3.2 In all ships, where the distance from sea level to the point of access to, or egress from, the ship exceeds 9 m, and when it is intended to embark and disembark pilots by means of the accommodation ladder,[†] or other equally safe and convenient means in conjunction with a pilot ladder, the ship shall carry such equipment on each side, unless the equipment is capable of being transferred for use on either side.

---

[*] Refer to the recommendations by the International Organization for Standardization, in particular publication ISO 799:2004, *Ships and marine technology – Pilot ladders*.

[†] Refer to regulation II-1/3-9 on Means of embarkation on and disembarkation from ships, adopted by resolution MSC.256(84), together with the associated Guidelines (MSC.1/Circ.1331).

3.3 Safe and convenient access to, and egress from, the ship shall be provided by either:

.1 a pilot ladder requiring a climb of not less than 1.5 m and not more than 9 m above the surface of the water so positioned and secured that:

.1 it is clear of any possible discharges from the ship;

.2 it is within the parallel body length of the ship and, as far as is practicable, within the mid-ship half length of the ship;

.3 each step rests firmly against the ship's side; where constructional features, such as rubbing bands, would prevent the implementation of this provision, special arrangements shall, to the satisfaction of the Administration, be made to ensure that persons are able to embark and disembark safely;

.4 the single length of pilot ladder is capable of reaching the water from the point of access to, or egress from, the ship and due allowance is made for all conditions of loading and trim of the ship, and for an adverse list of 15°; the securing strong point, shackles and securing ropes shall be at least as strong as the side ropes; or

.2 an accommodation ladder in conjunction with the pilot ladder (i.e. a combination arrangement), or other equally safe and convenient means, whenever the distance from the surface of the water to the point of access to the ship is more than 9 m. The accommodation ladder shall be sited leading aft. When in use, means shall be provided to secure the lower platform of the accommodation ladder to the ship's side, so as to ensure that the lower end of the accommodation ladder and the lower platform are held firmly against the ship's side within the parallel body length of the ship and, as far as is practicable, within the mid-ship half length and clear of all discharges.

.1 when a combination arrangement is used for pilot access, means shall be provided to secure the pilot ladder and manropes to the ship's side at a point of nominally 1.5 m above the bottom platform of the accommodation ladder. In the case of a combination arrangement using an accommodation ladder with a trapdoor in the bottom platform (i.e. embarkation platform), the pilot ladder and man ropes shall be rigged through the trapdoor extending above the platform to the height of the handrail.

4   Access to the ship's deck

Means shall be provided to ensure safe, convenient and unobstructed passage for any person embarking on, or disembarking from, the ship between the head of the pilot ladder, or of any accommodation ladder or other appliance, and the ship's deck. Where such passage is by means of:

.1   a gateway in the rails or bulwark, adequate handholds shall be provided;

.2   a bulwark ladder, two handhold stanchions rigidly secured to the ship's structure at or near their bases and at higher points shall be fitted. The bulwark ladder shall be securely attached to the ship to prevent overturning.

5   Shipside doors

Shipside doors used for pilot transfer shall not open outwards.

6   Mechanical pilot hoists

Mechanical pilot hoists shall not be used.

7   Associated equipment

7.1   The following associated equipment shall be kept at hand ready for immediate use when persons are being transferred:

.1   two man-ropes of not less than 28 mm and not more than 32 mm in diameter properly secured to the ship if required by the pilot; man-ropes shall be fixed at the rope end to the ring plate fixed on deck and shall be ready for use when the pilot disembarks, or upon request from a pilot approaching to board (the manropes shall reach the height of the stanchions or bulwarks at the point of access to the deck before terminating at the ring plate on deck);

.2   a lifebuoy equipped with a self-igniting light;

.3   a heaving line.

7.2   When required by paragraph 4 above, stanchions and bulwark ladders shall be provided.

8 Lighting

Adequate lighting shall be provided to illuminate the transfer arrangements overside and the position on deck where a person embarks or disembarks."

Appendix
Certificates

Form of Safety Certificate for Passenger Ships

11 *The following new paragraphs 2.10 and 2.11 are added after the existing paragraph 2.9:*

"2.10 the ship was/was not[1] subject to alternative design and arrangements in pursuance of regulation(s) II-1/55 / II-2/17 / III/38[1] of the Convention;

2.11 a Document of approval of alternative design and arrangements for machinery and electrical installations/fire protection/life-saving appliances[1] is/is not[1] appended to this Certificate.

---

[1] Delete as appropriate."

Form of Safety Construction Certificate for Cargo Ships

12 *The following new paragraphs 4 and 5 are added after the existing paragraph 3:*

"4 That the ship was/was not[4] subject to alternative design and arrangements in pursuance of regulation(s) II-1/55 / II-2/17[4] of the Convention.

5 That a Document of approval of alternative design and arrangements for machinery and electrical installations/fire protection[4] is/is not[4] appended to this Certificate.

---

[4] Delete as appropriate."

Form of Safety Equipment Certificate for Cargo Ships

13   *The following new paragraphs 2.7 and 2.8 are added after the existing paragraph 2.6:*

"2.7   the ship was/was not[4] subject to alternative design and arrangements in pursuance of regulation(s) II-2/17 / III/38[4] of the Convention;

2.8   a Document of approval of alternative design and arrangements for fire protection/life-saving appliances[4] is/is not[4] appended to this Certificate.

---

[4] Delete as appropriate."

Form of Nuclear Passenger Ship Safety Certificate

14   *The existing paragraphs 2.11 and 2.12 are replaced by the following:*

"2.11   the ship was/was not[1] subject to alternative design and arrangements in pursuance of regulation(s) II-1/55 / II-2/17 / III/38[1] of the Convention;

2.12   a Document of approval of alternative design and arrangements for machinery and electrical installations/fire protection/life-saving appliances[1] is/is not[1] appended to this Certificate.

---

[1] Delete as appropriate."

Form of Nuclear Cargo Ship Safety Certificate

15   *The existing paragraphs 2.10 and 2.11 are replaced by the following:*

"2.10   the ship was/was not[3] subject to alternative design and arrangements in pursuance of regulation(s) II-1/55 / II-2/17 / III/38/[3] of the Convention;

2.11   a Document of approval of alternative design and arrangements for machinery and electrical installations/fire protection/life-saving appliances[3] is/is not[3] appended to this Certificate.

---

[3] Delete as appropriate."

Resolution MSC.309(88)

(adopted on 3 December 2010)

Amendments to the Protocol of 1988 relating to the International Convention for the Safety of Life at Sea, 1974

THE MARITIME SAFETY COMMITTEE,

RECALLING Article 28(b) of the Convention on the International Maritime Organization concerning the functions of the Committee,

RECALLING FURTHER article VIII(b) of the International Convention for the Safety of Life at Sea (SOLAS), 1974 (hereinafter referred to as "the Convention") and article VI of the Protocol of 1988 relating to the Convention (hereinafter referred to as "the 1988 SOLAS Protocol") concerning the procedure for amending the 1988 SOLAS Protocol,

HAVING CONSIDERED, at its eighty-eighth session, amendments to the 1988 SOLAS Protocol proposed and circulated in accordance with article VIII(b)(i) of the Convention and article VI of the 1988 SOLAS Protocol,

1.   ADOPTS, in accordance with article VIII(b)(iv) of the Convention and article VI of the 1988 SOLAS Protocol, amendments to the appendix to the Annex to the 1988 SOLAS Protocol, the text of which is set out in the Annex to the present resolution;

2.   DETERMINES, in accordance with article VIII(b)(vi)(2)(bb) of the Convention and article VI of the 1988 SOLAS Protocol, that the said amendments shall be deemed to have been accepted on 1 January 2012, unless, prior to that date, more than one third of the Parties to the 1988 SOLAS Protocol or Parties the combined merchant fleets of which constitute not less than 50% of the gross tonnage of the world's merchant fleet, have notified their objections to the amendments;

3.   INVITES the Parties concerned to note that, in accordance with article VIII(b)(vii)(2) of the Convention and article VI of the 1988 SOLAS Protocol, the amendments shall enter into force on 1 July 2012, upon their acceptance in accordance with paragraph 2 above;

4.   REQUESTS the Secretary-General, in conformity with article VIII(b)(v) of the Convention and article VI of the 1988 SOLAS Protocol, to transmit certified copies of the present resolution and the text of the amendments contained in the Annex to all Parties to the 1988 SOLAS Protocol;

5.   FURTHER REQUESTS the Secretary-General to transmit copies of this resolution and its Annex to Members of the Organization, which are not Parties to the 1988 SOLAS Protocol.

Annex

Amendments to the Protocol of 1988 relating to the International Convention for the Safety of Life at Sea, 1974, as amended

Annex

Modifications and additions to the Annex to the International Convention for the Safety of Life at Sea, 1974

Appendix

Modifications and additions to the appendix to the Annex to the International Convention for the Safety of Life at Sea, 1974

Form of Safety Certificate for Passenger Ships

1   *The existing paragraphs 2.10 and 2.11 are replaced by the following:*

"2.10   the ship was/was not[1] subject to alternative design and arrangements in pursuance of regulation(s) II-1/55 / II-2/17 / III/38[1] of the Convention;

2.11   a Document of approval of alternative design and arrangements for machinery and electrical installations/fire protection/life-saving appliances[1] is/is not[1] appended to this Certificate.

------

[1] Delete as appropriate."

Form of Safety Construction Certificate for Cargo Ships

2   *The existing paragraphs 5 and 6 are replaced by the following:*

"5   That the ship was/was not[4] subject to alternative design and arrangements in pursuance of regulation(s) II-1/55 / II-2/17[4] of the Convention;

6   That a Document of approval of alternative design and arrangements for machinery and electrical installations/fire protection[4] is/is not[4] appended to this Certificate.

---

[4] Delete as appropriate."

Form of Safety Equipment Certificate for Cargo Ships

3   *The existing paragraphs 2.7 and 2.8 are replaced by the following:*

"2.7   the ship was/was not[4] subject to alternative design and arrangements in pursuance of regulation(s) II-2/17 / III/38[4] of the Convention;

2.8   a Document of approval of alternative design and arrangements for fire protection/life-saving appliances[4] is/is not[4] appended to this Certificate.

---

[4] Delete as appropriate."

Form of Safety Certificate for Cargo Ships

4   *The existing paragraphs 2.11 and 2.12 are replaced by the following:*

"2.11   the ship was/was not[4] subject to alternative design and arrangements in pursuance of regulation(s) II-1/55 / II-2/17 / III/38[4] of the Convention;

2.12   a Document of approval of alternative design and arrangements for machinery and electrical installations/fire protection/life-saving appliances[4] is/is not[4] appended to this Certificate.

---

[4] Delete as appropriate."

2011 amendments

The amendments presented in this section comprise
the annex to MSC.317(89) adopted in May 2011.

Resolution MSC.317(89)

(adopted on 20 May 2011)

Adoption of amendments to the International Convention for the Safety of Life at Sea, 1974, as amended

THE MARITIME SAFETY COMMITTEE,

RECALLING Article 28(b) of the Convention on the International Maritime Organization concerning the functions of the Committee,

RECALLING FURTHER article VIII(b) of the International Convention for the Safety of Life at Sea (SOLAS), 1974 (hereinafter referred to as "the Convention"), concerning the amendment procedure applicable to the Annex to the Convention, other than to the provisions of chapter I thereof,

HAVING CONSIDERED, at its eighty-ninth session, amendments to the Convention, proposed and circulated in accordance with article VIII(b)(i) thereof,

1.   ADOPTS, in accordance with article VIII(b)(iv) of the Convention, amendments to the Convention, the text of which is set out in the Annex to the present resolution;

2.   DETERMINES, in accordance with article VIII(b)(vi)(2)(bb) of the Convention, that the said amendments shall be deemed to have been accepted on 1 July 2012, unless, prior to that date, more than one third of the Contracting Governments to the Convention or Contracting Governments the combined merchant fleets of which constitute not less than 50% of the gross tonnage of the world's merchant fleet, have notified their objections to the amendments;

3.   INVITES SOLAS Contracting Governments to note that, in accordance with article VIII(b)(vii)(2) of the Convention, the amendments shall

enter into force on 1 January 2013 upon their acceptance in accordance with paragraph 2 above;

4.   REQUESTS the Secretary-General, in conformity with article VIII(b)(v) of the Convention, to transmit certified copies of the present resolution and the text of the amendments contained in the Annex to all Contracting Governments to the Convention;

5.   FURTHER REQUESTS the Secretary-General to transmit copies of this resolution and its Annex to Members of the Organization which are not Contracting Governments to the Convention.

Annex

Amendments to the International Convention for the Safety of Life at Sea, 1974, as amended

Chapter III
Life-saving appliances and arrangements

Regulation 1
Application

The following new paragraph 5 is added after the existing paragraph 4:

"**5** Notwithstanding paragraph 4.2, for all ships, not later than the first scheduled dry-docking after 1 July 2014, but not later than 1 July 2019, lifeboat on-load release mechanisms not complying with paragraphs 4.4.7.6.4 to 4.4.7.6.6 of the Code shall be replaced with equipment that complies with the Code.[*]

---

[*] Refer to the Guidelines for evaluation and replacement of lifeboat release and retrieval systems (MSC.1/Circ.1392)."

Notes

Notes

Notes

Notes